Really Short Walks
near Ingleborough

Paul White

Whinray Books · Ilkley

All the walks in this book were checked prior to publication, at which time the instructions were correct. However, changes can occur in the countryside over which neither the author nor the publisher has any control. Please let us know if you encounter any serious problems.

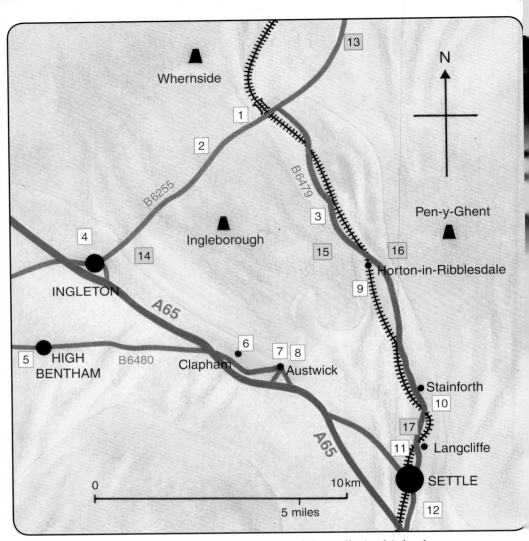

The approximate locations of the walks in this book

First published 2015
Whinray Books is an imprint of Bossiney Books Ltd,
33 Queens Drive, Ilkley, LS29 9QW
www.bossineybooks.com

© 2015 Paul White   All rights reserved

ISBN 978-0-9571939-2-5

Acknowledgements
The maps are by Graham Hallowell. All photographs are by the author.
Printed in Great Britain by R Booth Ltd, Penryn, Cornwall

Introduction

The delightful walks in this book are from 3.5 to 5.8km (2 1/4 to 3 1/2 miles) in length. Some are easy, others short but quite challenging. All have been chosen to show the variety and interest of the Ingleborough area. We have not suggested how long they will take, because readers' walking abilities will vary considerably, nor have we selected these walks with pushchairs or wheelchairs in mind: most would be unsuitable on this often rugged terrain.

The Ingleborough area is an extraordinary landscape, renowned among geologists for its limestone, shaped by the Craven Fault system and by repeated glaciation. For me, it's a place of childhood memories and the knowledge that my ancestors farmed here over many centuries. There are plenty of abandoned or converted farms, ruined barns and tottering stone walls which give a glimpse of an ancient and very tough way of life – not altogether gone, because there are still many working farms, especially in the lower pastureland.

Safety (please take seriously!)

If you are safety-conscious you should have no problems, but you do need to go prepared. Some of these walks will take you into lonely places where mobile phones get no reception. Consult the weather forecast before you start, walk in company, let someone know where you are going.

You will need proper walking boots or shoes for grip and ankle support. Many walkers find a walking pole is a helpful accessory. The high ground will always be colder than the lowlands and wind chill is often a factor. You should always carry extra clothing in your rucksack as well as waterproofs. Hat and gloves may well be needed (sunhat in summer) and you should take a supply of water, because dehydration makes you tired, and some spare food.

Maps

The sketch-maps in this book are just that – sketches. You may want to take the Ordnance Survey's map OL2, which covers most of the area.

Consideration for the landscape and for farmers

Please keep to the paths. Keep dogs on leads especially during the lambing and nesting seasons. Leave gates as you find them.

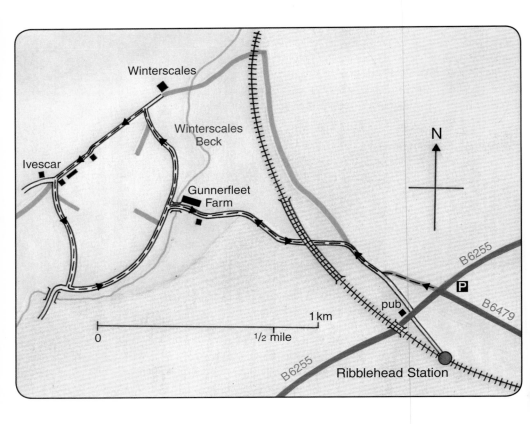

Walk 1   Ribblehead and Ivescar

Distance: 4.9 km (3 miles)
Character: An easy walk, nearly flat, and on solid farm tracks throughout, so a good choice after a period of heavy rain. With Ingleborough to one side and Whernside to the other, and the famous Ribblehead Viaduct apparently sealing one end, this flat valley bottom has a dramatic character.

You could arrive by train and start the walk from Ribblehead station. If arriving by car, park near the junction of B6479 and B6255.

Take the footpath (BLEAMOOR SIDINGS) towards the viaduct. Join a gravel track and follow it under the viaduct, then on to Gunnerfleet Farm. Cross Winterscales Beck and turn right. On reaching a T-junction, turn left, PUBLIC BRIDLEWAY STAR END.

In the first field on your left, notice the numerous shake holes. These hollows occur where the surface clay is washed down into a fissure in the limestone beneath.

At Ivescar Farm turn left, PUBLIC BRIDLEWAY WINTERSCALES BECK. At a track junction just before you reach the beck, turn sharp left through a field gate, RIBBLEHEAD.

When you reach Gunnerfleet Farm, turn right across the bridge and retrace your steps to the start.

The Ribblehead Viaduct

Strangely, this extraordinary achievement of the railway age seems to fit in with the landscape, possibly because, impressive though it is in Victorian engineering terms, it remains dwarfed by the mountains. It was constructed between 1870 and 1875, when a temporary small town housed around 1000 people – the workers and their families, and those who supplied their needs. The 'town' was subdivided on class lines, into areas wittily known as Belgravia and Sebastopol: very little remains.

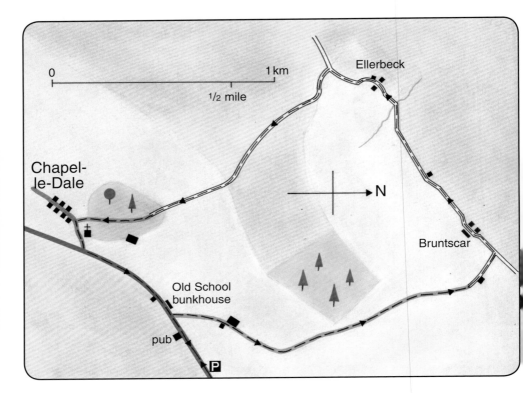

Walk 2 Chapel-le-Dale

Distance: 5.8 km (3 1/2 miles)
Character: Majestic scenery all around, ending in the beautiful
wooded hamlet of Chapel-le-Dale. Most of the walk is on good
tarmac or gravel farm tracks, but there is a section of the
relatively busy B6255, so you might think twice if you have
children or dogs with you.

Starting point: Ideally you would park on the roadside opposite
the little church of Chapel-le-Dale – saving a few hundred metres
of road walking and putting the climb at the beginning of the
walk rather than the end – but there is space there for only two
cars, so probably you will need to park on the roadside uphill
from The Old Hill Inn, and the instructions will start from there.

Walk back past the inn. Just before the Old School building, turn
sharp right on a gated lane. Follow the lane across the valley

bottom, until it becomes a gravel farm track. At a T-junction, turn left (PUBLIC BRIDLEWAY SCAR END) and pass Bruntscar Hall.

Follow the track to Ellerbeck Farm, bear left in the farmyard and continue along a track when you leave the farm.

At a cattle grid beside a row of conifers, turn left on a track which winds gently down and enters woodland. Pass a statue with a story to tell, and enter the hamlet of Chapel-le-Dale. Reaching a lane junction by the church, turn left out to the main road.

Now for the hard bit! You need to ascend the slope for about 800 m, taking great care because of the traffic. But at least you have the prospect of slaking your thirst at the pub – unless, as I did, you go on a Monday when the pub is closed. In my case, a bitter non-experience.

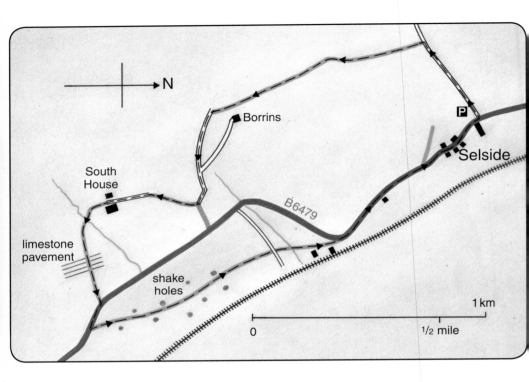

Walk 3 Selside

Distance: 5.2 km (3¹/₄ miles)
*Character: Hill farming country, with lovely views, but showing
examples of limestone outcrops and shake holes. Fairly gentle
walking for the most part. There are two short stretches of a
moderately busy road: be prepared to stand on the verge, out of
the way of traffic.*

Park just north of Selside, along a stony track leading off the
B6479. Walk away from the road and after 400 m turn left on a
grassy track. When this ends, continue ahead with the wall on
your right. When the wall ends, bear left across the field to a
ladder stile.

Cross the stile, and continue towards the far left corner of the
next field. Straight ahead you will see another ladder stile. Cross
and continue in the same direction, this time with the wall on
your left.

Meeting a cross track, turn left through a gate, and follow the track, which is joined by another track and then swings right. At a junction continue ahead and follow the tarmac track up to a farm. Pass through the yard, then turn left through a field gate and descend to a way-marked stile. Cross the beck and the stile, and turn left to cross another stile.

The next field is difficult, as the path is not obvious. Head east if you have a compass, or towards the northern slope of Pen-y-ghent if not. Either way you'll need to pick your way carefully through some outcrops of limestone pavement. Descend to the road and turn right along it.

After 280 m, turn sharp left over a stile, PUBLIC FOOTPATH SELSIDE. Watch out for shake holes and thistles. Continue in the direction indicated, crossing fields and stiles, then a track. After crossing a streamlet, climb the hillock ahead, then keep the wall on your right till you reach the road at Selside Cottages.

Turn right along the road, through the hamlet of Selside, back to the parking place.

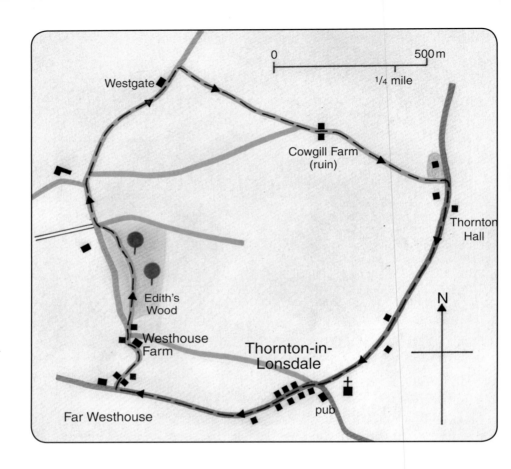

Walk 4 Thornton-in-Lonsdale

Distance: 3.8 km (2¼ miles)
*Character: A walk in a farming area on the lower slopes of the
upland. This walk has been planned for people who prefer very
quiet lanes rather than fields, though an alternative version could
be walked using more field footpaths – see the OS map.*

Start from Thornton-in-Lonsdale church. From the lych-gate,
turn right past the Marton Arms and at the lane junction turn
left. Follow this lane out of Thornton to the next hamlet, Far
Westhouse. Turn right on a side road, and follow it up past
Westhouse Farm.

A gate on the right leads into Edith's Wood, which is a fairly

10

new plantation of indigenous trees. Unless you want to use the lane, follow the permissive path through the wood and leave by a stile at the upper end. Turn right onto the lane.

Keep right at the next lane junction and climb past a farm before turning right on a footpath, WEST VIEW. Cross the stile then keep the wall on your left. The views get even finer as Ingleborough comes in sight. Keeping the wall on your left, go through fields and a new plantation, crossing three more stiles, before descending to Cowgill Farm, where the house is a ruin.

Cross a beck, likely to be dry in summer, walk between the buildings, cross a ladder stile at the far end, and walk ahead to cross the next stile.

Now head diagonally right: once at the top of the slope, you will see a group of buildings. Head just to the right of the group, to a field gate at the right-hand end of a clump of trees.

Cross a stile beside the gate and walk along the track to the lane. Turn right and follow the lane back down to the church.

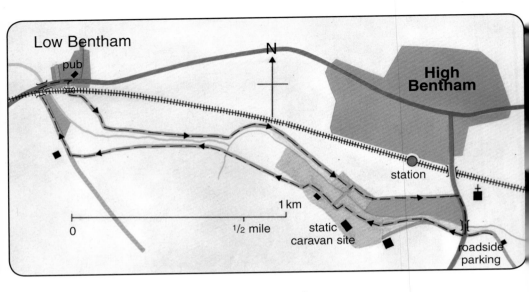

Walk 5   The Wenning at Bentham

Distance: 5 km (3 miles)

Character: A walk between High and Low Bentham, along the River Wenning, which is placid in summer – though not always in winter. The landscape is charming, if less dramatic than most other walks in this book; there is a stretch through a caravan site, but the riverside paths compensate.

To get there: Take Station Road from the centre of High Bentham, descend past the station, cross the river bridge and turn left along a lane. There is roadside parking when the lane bends right.

Walk back to the bridge and cross into the private road opposite. At a cattle grid, bear right on the footpath. Enter a caravan park, where the signage is limited. Start by heading parallel to the river and when this is no longer possible turn left, then right along the main drive, passing a block of bathing and toilet facilities.

Then turn left, up a narrow path, PUBLIC FOOTPATH TO LOW BENTHAM THROUGH KISSING GATE. This winds through trees and out to a meadow. Keep the hedge on your right, then turn right across a stile and a tributary stream.

Now at last you can walk along the Wenning bank, before

climbing higher and walking parallel to the river. On reaching a lane, turn right and walk into Low Bentham. Go under the railway and turn right on the main road. Just before a road junction and The Sundial inn, turn right (PUBLIC FOOTPATH), go back under the railway and bear left, past a fish farm.

Now follow the riverside path back to High Bentham. You will re-enter the caravan park, which is on both sides of the river. This time follow the main drive, parallel to the river. When you reach a T-junction by a bridge, turn left, and then shortly right. This leads to a lane. Turn left along the lane.

The older terraces were housing for workers at the former mill, now replaced by modern housing. Bentham's mills at various times produced cotton and silk, but are more famous for weaving flax into firemen's hosepipes – a technique apparently invented in Bentham.

When you reach the T-junction opposite the early Victorian church (closed at the time of writing) turn right back to the river bridge.

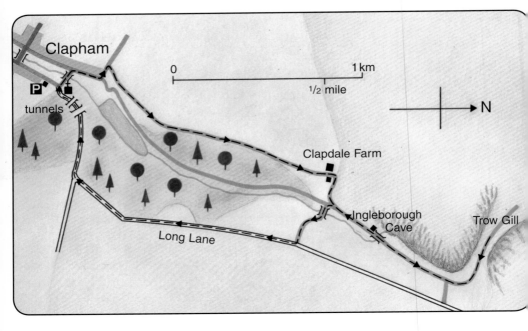

Walk 6 Clapham and Trow Gill

*Distance: The basic circular walk is 4 km (2 1/2 miles) with
an optional extension of a further 2 km (1 1/4 miles) to pass
Ingleborough Cave (an impressive show cave) and see Trow Gill.
Character: There are two very different versions of this walk.
The circular walk has attractive limestone scenery either side of
Clapdale, but there are two steep ascents, and one steep descent.*

*The alternative there-and-back route through the Ingleborough
Estate (small fee) is shorter, very pretty, and has no serious
ascents or descents, having been designed for genteel Victorians to
walk beside the artificial lake. Either way you have an optional
extension through a glacial meltwater valley to a former waterfall
at Trow Gill (see photo opposite).*

Start from the church at Clapham and walk down across the
stream. Turn right. At the entrance to the Ingleborough Estate,
for the alternative route, walk ahead, small fee. Otherwise turn
left. After about 100 m turn right up a track, BW INGLEBOROUGH
CAVE.

14

Follow the track up to and through Clapdale Farm, and once through the farmyard turn right, steeply downhill.

Reaching the track along the valley bottom, EITHER for Trow Gill turn left and follow the track past the Cave, then after 800 m go through a gate to see the foot of the waterfall, created when a huge Ice Age glacier melted very fast. Then retrace your steps.

OR, for the short route, turn right along the track, and very shortly left on a path across a footbridge. Climb steeply up the other side, then cross a stile onto Long Lane. Turn right and follow the track to a T-junction. Turn right again, and descend through tunnels back to Clapham Church.

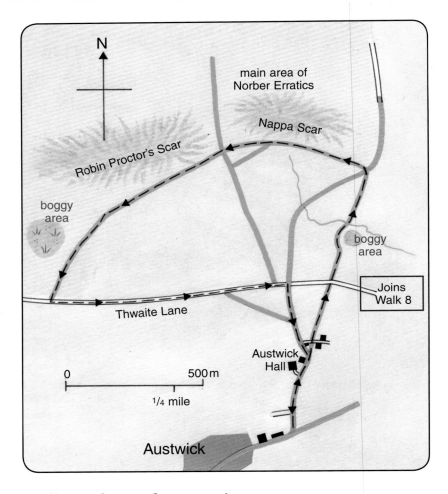

Walk 7   The Norber Erratics

Distance: 4 km (2½ miles) plus exploration of the erratics.
Character: A visit to some of the most extraordinary geological
features of the Dales, with lovely views as a bonus. Quite steep
in places, with many high stiles, and you will need to watch your
footing. See page 32 for background information on this walk.

Start from Austwick. Drive past the Game Cock and then the
school. Take the first left, Townhead Lane, and park in the street.
Walk up the street, past Austwick Hall. After wet weather, continue up the lane, because the footpath route can be quite boggy.

If the weather has been fairly dry, turn right 40 m beyond

Austwick Hall into a drive and immediately left along PUBLIC FOOTPATH. Cross a drive, climb a stile and walk up the field with a wall on your right. At the top, cross Thwaite Lane by two stiles. Continue down a field with the wall on your right. After another stile, cross a stream by a plank bridge and follow a beaten path up to a stile.

Cross the lane and take the footpath, NORBER. Keep the wall on your right. You will pass along the side of a cliff, Nappa Scar, immediately beside a famous geological 'unconformity'.

Follow the path through a wall and up to a stile. The field you now enter contains many of the 'Norber Erratics'. Explore the area above for as long as you want, then return to the stile.

Return to the wall, and turn right. Follow the wall down steep rocks, then bear right towards a cliff – Robin Proctor's Scar. At a signpost continue ahead, CLAPHAM, with a wall to your left. Shortly after a stile, the path bears diagonally left, skirts a bog to the right, and reaches a ladder stile. Cross the stile and turn left along Thwaite Lane.

Ignore a footpath to the right. On reaching a tarmac lane, turn right downhill back towards the village.

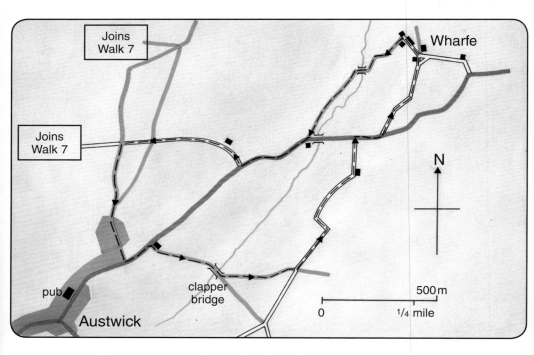

Walk 8 Austwick and Wharfe

Distance: 4.2 km (2 1/2 miles)
*Character: A delightful walk, almost flat except for the final
stretch (which you can omit if you wish) and with stunning
scenery all around. Most of the walk is on ancient enclosed
trackways, which were once the main routes of the area and are
probably little changed since the eighteenth century. In those days
you were unlikely to meet a motor caravan or an oil delivery
vehicle, but travellers grumbled about having to pass trains of
packhorses with their wide panniers!*

Park near the foot of Townhead Lane. Walk to the foot of the
street and turn left. After 130 m turn right along a track, PENNINE
BRIDLEWAY FEIZOR.

 Cross a stream by a clapper bridge beside a ford. After another
25 m, turn left over a stile and cross the field diagonally by a well
beaten path. (Alternatively, continue up the track and turn left
at the next junction.)

18

At the far top corner of the field, cross a stile, turn left along a track and almost immediately keep left. The track zig-zags then leads to a farm. Bear left along the farm access drive.

At the road turn right, then take the first track on the left, which leads up to Wharfe. Within the hamlet keep left, then left again, along a level street. At the far end, by LOW HOUSE FARM, turn left down an enclosed path.

Follow the main path as it winds out to the lane. Turn right, and follow the lane for 300m, then turn right, PENNINE BRIDLEWAY CLAPHAM. (Alternatively you could continue along the lane, which is both shorter and saves a climb of about 30 m, 100 ft.)

The path climbs gently to a lane. Turn left here, and descend Townhead Lane back to the starting point.

This walk can easily be combined with Walk 7, or extended very simply to visit the Norber Erratics.

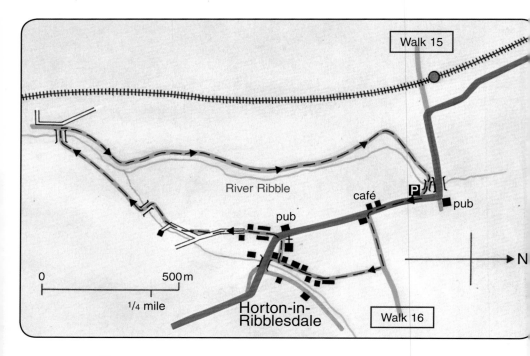

Walk 9   A Horton-in-Ribblesdale circuit

Distance: 3.5 km (2 1/4 miles)
*Character: A nearly flat walk, very easy except for 50 m of
slightly uneven walking at one point. Meadows, a pleasant riverside path, and finally an attractive hidden part of the village.*

Start from the church gate. (There is some parking in a trun-
cated section of old road just the other side of the bridge, or
parking at the Golden Lion.) Facing the Golden Lion, turn left
and take the minor road between houses, FOOTPATH TAY BRIDGE.

Pass the village hall and continue along a gravel track. After a
bend in the track, bear right (PUBLIC FOOTPATH) and soon briefly
join an access track, then continue in the same direction when
it turns left.

Turn left across a footbridge, then immediately right. Cross
the field heading south-west. A gate beside the river leads to a
footbridge. Cross and turn right along the bankside footpath,
RIBBLE WAY. Follow the waymarks.

20

Approaching Horton, the river bends right, and the path does likewise, entering a riverside field. Walk the length of the field with the river on your right, then climb steps at the end. Turn right and cross a footbridge to the main car park, with WC.

Turn right out of the car park along the main road, passing the Pen-y-ghent Café, then turn left on a track, PENNINE WAY. Climb gently. At a track junction, turn right. The track becomes a lane, with interesting vernacular buildings.

When you reach the churchyard, turn right through it, back to the starting point.

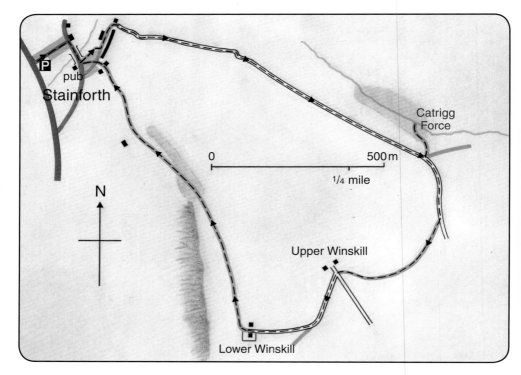

Walk 10   Stainforth and Catrigg Force

Distance: 3.75 km (2 1/4 miles)
Character: Stunning scenery throughout. The route includes a visit to Catrigg Force (a.k.a. Catrigg Foss), a beautiful waterfall in a woodland setting. Quite a strenuous walk, with a steep climb at the beginning, and a tricky descent towards the end, for which you need to be sure-footed. (Reversing the direction of the walk makes it easier, but less dramatic.)

Start from the car park in Stainforth. Turn right out of the car park. At the T-junction turn right across the bridge, then turn left on a path beside the stream, FP MAIN STREET 40 YDS. Reaching Main Street (actually a lane) turn left and walk up to a green, then turn right uphill.

The lane soon becomes a track enclosed by walls. Follow it uphill until it arrives at a gate. Turn left (CATRIGG FOSS ONLY) on a path down to the foot of the waterfall.

Retrace your steps to the track and go through the field gate. Follow the gravel track uphill and through a gate, then immediately bear right across the field, PENNINE BRIDLEWAY WINSKILL. Join a track and go through a gate. Follow the track to a track junction at High Winskill.

Take the PUBLIC FOOTPATH ahead (actually a farm track) across a cattle grid and down to Lower Winskill Farm. Pass through the yard and across a paddock to a ladder stile. Climb the bank, then bear right on a well-beaten grassy path which leads through a gap in a wall. Don't let the stunnng view distract you: the path is uneven, and it would be easy to stumble.

Another ladder stile leads into woodland, and you descend Stainforth Crag down a very tricky stepped path, with a drop to your left. Take great care! Emerging from the wood, continue in the same direction downhill, following waymarks.

Leave the field by a gate and continue downhill to cross a stile. Turn left at 'Ingle Byre'. At the lane turn right and immediately left, to the Craven Heifer. Turn right across the bridge and retrace your steps to the car park.

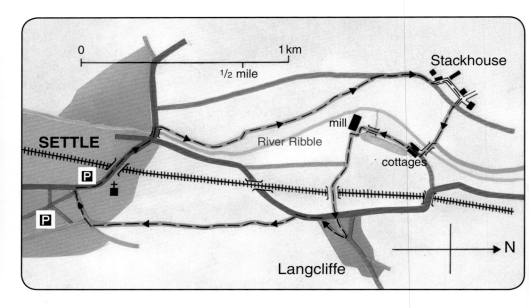

Walk 11 Stackhouse and Langcliffe

Distance: 5 km (3 1/4 miles)
Character: An easy fairly level walk with valley views, taking in an interesting former cotton-spinning, and later paper, mill and its mill pond, and then the lovely village of Langcliffe.

Start from Settle Market Place. Take the main road north, downhill to pass the church and under the railway. Cross the river bridge then turn right on PUBLIC FOOTPATH RIBBLE WAY STACKHOUSE. Follow the path till it reaches a lane, then turn right along it.

After passing the Stackhouse Old Hall, turn left on a track, PUBLIC BRIDLEWAY. Turn right at CARRHOLME then right again at a junction, which will bring you back to the lane. Turn left and immediately right, PUBLIC FOOTPATH RIBBLE WAY STAINFORTH. At a T-junction turn right, then immediately left over a footbridge.

Turn right between terraces of cottages, then left on a footpath as signed. This soon turns right and runs alongside the mill pond – which was the subject of a legal dispute as far back as 1221. At the mill, follow the path round the side of the mill then

24

Above:
Langcliffe
village

Below:
Langcliffe Mill,
seen on the
way out from
Settle

out to a lane. Cross the lane and take the enclosed path, over the railway and up to the main road.

Cross the road and take the passage ahead, to explore Langcliffe's peaceful central space. Then return to the main road and turn left along the footway. After 200 m turn left along a lane with a dead-end sign.

Follow the lane – which was formerly the road from upper Ribblesdale into Settle – until it suddenly turns right. Keep ahead downhill into the Market Place.

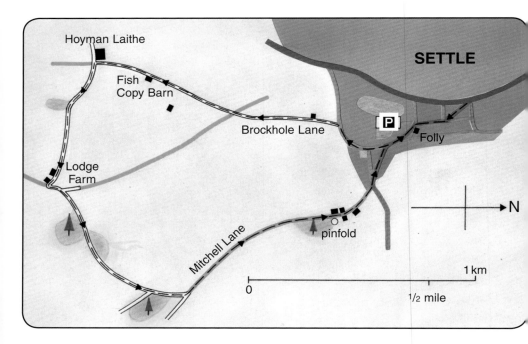

Walk 12   South from Settle

Distance: 4.75 km (3 miles)
Character: A splendid walk for scenery and historical interest:
historic parts of Settle, a lane through lowland pastures, then
a steady climb (120 m, nearly 400 ft) to the high moor, before a
dramatic descent back to the town. The enclosed tracks can be
muddy or covered by puddles after rain.

Start from the fountain in the Market Square. Take the diagonal
road across the square and continue past the Talbot Arms, then
bear left to the Folly (the Museum of North Craven Life) and
immediately right, VICTORIA STREET.

When the 'main' road bears left and uphill, continue ahead
on the level. Pass The Green and follow the lane downhill.
Immediately after LOWER GREENFOOT turn left onto an enclosed
track.

After some distance, continue ahead through a gate at a footpath junction. Meeting a farm track, turn left uphill.

26

At Lodge Farm, pass the barn and the house, go through a 7-bar gate and turn left along the track. After 100 m, at a fork bear right uphill. After passing plantations on either side, continue ahead at a track junction, then turn left at a T-junction, PENNINE BRIDLEWAY SETTLE.

This lane was, until about 1753, the main road from Long Preston into Settle – the equivalent of the A65. Whether you had been travelling from York to Lancaster, or from Halifax to Kendal, this is the route you would have followed – but of course the surface would not have been tarmac!

On the long steep descent you will have wonderful views over the town and the surrounding hills. The first structure as you enter the town is the pinfold, now a picnic spot, where stray animals were once impounded.

At a road junction, bear right downhill. At JUNCTION LODGE bear left, and retrace your steps to the start.

There-and-back walks

Walk 13   Gearstones and the Roman road

This walk uses a very well maintained track, and will generally be dry underfoot. It therefore makes a good winter walk – but you need to wrap up very warmly as it is extremely exposed.

Park just to the west of Gearstones. Walk with care along the road in the Hawes direction until you reach a sharp bend. Keep right through a gate (DALES WAY FOOTPATH TO CAM END) and follow the track down over the river. Climb steadily. Once the track bends to the left, you are on the line of the Roman military road from Lancaster to Bainbridge in Wensleydale. As you climb, a glorious view opens up behind you, with the Ribblehead Viaduct in the distance, between Ingleborough to the left and Whernside to the right.

Walk 14　Ingleton to Crina Bottom

This is the route from Ingleton up Ingleborough, so it's quite a climb. You might want to go as far as Crina Bottom Farm, about halfway up. The route is a stony farm track, so it is mainly dry, though after heavy rain puddles may form right across the track in a couple of places.

Do wrap up warm, because you will be exposed to wind.

Start from the village up the Hawes Road, B6255. Shortly after the junction with the Clapham Old Road, keep right, FP INGLEBOROUGH. Climb steeply. The first five minutes of the climb are the worst!

Before long the track becomes walled on both sides. Follow it to a gate, then for another 300 m and you will have a splendid view of Ingleborough.

Walk 15   Horton-in-Ribblesdale to Sulber Nick

A gentle steady climb up to a plateau, to see Sulber Nick – a long thin geological fault line like a shallow valley.

If starting from the car park at Horton, take the footpath in front of the public conveniences to cross the Ribble by a foot-bridge, then turn left beside the main road.

Continue ahead at the station, cross the tracks and take the footpath – it's one of the main routes up Ingleborough (probably the easiest, though also the longest) so it's well used.

To your left you will see Horton Quarry with its extraordinarily coloured pond.

At a path junction with a mini cairn, turn left as marked. At the next path junction continue ahead, INGLEBOROUGH. Go through a gate into Sulber Nick.

Walk 16   From Horton towards Pen-y-ghent

This is the beginning of the main route up Pen-y-Ghent, which in all is about 11 km there-and-back: you can go as far as you want.

Start from the car park at Horton-in-Ribblesdale. Turn right along the main road, passing the Pen-y-ghent Café, then turn left on a track, PENNINE WAY. Climb gently. At a junction, bear left.

Opposite:
Horton Quarry
pond, seen on
Walk 15

Above right:
Pen-y-ghent,
seen from
Walk 16

Below right:
The Ribble near
Langcliffe, seen
on Walk 17

Walk 17 The river at Langcliffe

Start from the car park at Langcliffe, opposite the church. Walk back to the centre of the village, and bear right past the war memorial along NEW STREET. Turn right along the pavement of the main road. Cross the railway and immediately turn left down a lane. Just before a terrace of houses, turn right across a footbridge. On the far side, turn right and keep right along the bankside path, which after just over 2 km leads to the rapids called Stainforth Force. Return by the route on page 24.

Some notes on Walk 7 (page 16)

The Norber Erratics

These are boulders carried by an ancient glacier and deposited on other rocks, which have subsequently eroded beneath them.

The Nappa Scar unconformity (photo above)

An 'unconformity' occurs where rocks of various geological eras occur in unexpected ways, for example if a whole era is missing. At Norber, the upper layers are Carboniferous, the lower layers Ordovician. The Devonian is totally missing (unsurprising since the area was never below sea level in this period so no rocks were laid down) and the Silurian is represented only by a layer, averaging a metre deep, of jumbled Silurian pebbles and boulders (see photo above). Not being a geologist, I can't explain it!

Robin Proctor's Scar

Legend has it that Robin Proctor was a local farmer who liked his drink, and often allowed his horse to take him from the pub back to his farm: one night he and his horse fell off the top of the cliff.

Thwaite Lane

This is a medieval through route, particularly important to that economic powerhouse Fountains Abbey. The road was walled in, following an Enclosure Act of 1758.